A guide to

RAM.
AND FAJ I ING

DR. MUSHARAF HUSSAIN
AND
DR. ABIA AFSAR-SIDDIQUI

Ta-Ha Publishers Ltd.

Written by: Dr. Musharaf Hussain and Dr. Abia Afsar-Siddiqui
Edited by: Abdassamad Clarke

A catalogue record of this book is available from the British Library.

ISBN-13: 978 1842000 79 3

Cover and Book design by Shakir Abdulcadir. opensquares.co.uk
Printed and bound by Mega Print, Turkey.

Cover Photo, The Alhambra, Spain © Shakir Abdulcadir

Table of Contents

1

THE VIRTUES OF RAMADAN

RAMADAN (literally meaning heat and dryness in Arabic) is the ninth month of the Islamic calendar entirely devoted to committed *ibadah* (worship) including *sawm* (fasting). Fasting during the month of Ramadan was first prescribed in the second year of Hijrah:

يَٰٓأَيُّهَا ٱلَّذِينَ ءَامَنُوا۟ كُتِبَ عَلَيْكُمُ ٱلصِّيَامُ
كَمَا كُتِبَ عَلَى ٱلَّذِينَ مِن قَبْلِكُمْ لَعَلَّكُمْ تَتَّقُونَ

You who have *iman*! Fasting is prescribed for you, as it was prescribed for those before you – so that hopefully you will have *taqwa*. (2:183)

فَمَن شَهِدَ مِنكُمُ ٱلشَّهْرَ فَلْيَصُمْهُ

...Any of you who are resident for the month should fast it. (2:185)

Ramadan is the springtime of the Islamic year. Just as the earth comes into bloom in spring, so the spiritual side of our nature is renewed and refreshed in Ramadan. This is a time for reflection, intense worship and strengthening family and community ties. This is a time when the mosques are thronging with people and there is a feeling of warmth, compassion and joy in the air. Muslims look forward to Ramadan because it brings with it the numerous blessings of Allah. Describing this prosperous time of worship, Abu Huraira 🕮 narrated that the Messenger of Allah 🕮 said:

> Ramadan a blessed month has come to you, whose fasting Allah has made obligatory for you, in which the gates of Heaven are opened and the gates of Jahim are locked, and the rebellious shayateen are chained up. Allah has in it a night which is better than a thousand months and whoever is deprived of it has certainly been deprived. (An-Nasa'i and Ahmad)

Since fasting is no ordinary act of worship, the potential rewards are also exceptional. The Messenger of Allah 🕮 said:

> Allah says, 'All the deeds of the son of Adam are for him: the good deeds will be multiplied ten times to seven hundred times, except fasting, which is for Me and I will reward him for it accordingly. He abandons his (sexual) desire, food and drink for Me.' (Muslim)

Allah is most generous in bestowing His favours upon the fasting person in the month of Ramadan and the Prophet 🕮 mentions five special favours of Allah. Abu Huraira 🕮 reported the Messenger of Allah 🕮 as having said:

> My community has been given five qualities in Ramadan which no community before it has been given: the bad breath of the fasting person is more fragrant to Allah than the scent of musk, the angels seek forgiveness for them until they break the fast, and Allah beautifies His Garden every day..., and in it the rebellious shayateen are shackled..., and they are forgiven in the last night. (Ahmad)

The first favour is that the bad breath coming from the mouth of the fasting person is better than musk, a valuable perfume. There are three commonly accepted interpretations to this point. One is that in the Hereafter Allah will reward the person who fasted with breath smelling of musk; or that on the Day of Judgement the one who fasted will be raised with their breath smelling of musk; or simply that in this world, to Allah the smell from the mouth of the fasting person is sweeter than the smell of musk, purely out of love for His obedient fasting servant.

The second favour is that, by Allah's command, the angels make *du'a* for the fasting person.

The third favour is that Allah adorns Heaven every day in anticipation of His servant, just as we might decorate our home in anticipation of a special guest.

The fourth favour, and an important feature of Ramadan, is that rebellious *shayateen* are chained. Some scholars are of the opinion that only the major *shayateen* are chained, while others believe that all of them are chained. Despite this reassurance, evil acts are still committed throughout Ramadan. A possible explanation for this is that, while the *shayateen* may indeed be chained, men who have acquired the characteristics of *shayateen*, by living a life full of wrong action, are still free to act as they please. Having committed wrong actions for the past eleven months, they will continue to do so during Ramadan because their hearts are blackened and they feel no remorse or shame.

The final favour is that Muslims are forgiven their wrong actions on having completed a Ramadan full of sincere *ibadah*.

Ramadan is also sometimes referred to as 'The Month of the Qur'an' because:

$$ شَهْرُ رَمَضَانَ ٱلَّذِىٓ أُنزِلَ فِيهِ ٱلْقُرْءَانُ هُدًى لِّلنَّاسِ $$

The month of Ramadan is the one in which the Qur'an was sent down as guidance for mankind,... (2:185)

$$ إِنَّآ أَنزَلْنَـٰهُ فِى لَيْلَةِ ٱلْقَدْرِ $$

Truly We sent it down on the Night of Power (*Laylat al–Qadr*). (97:1)

These *ayat* show the inseparable link between the Qur'an and Ramadan. It is said that 'Atiyya ibn al-Aswad once questioned Ibn Abbas 🙵 as to the explanation of these *ayat* since sections of the Qur'an are known to have been revealed in other months. Ibn Abbas 🙵 said, "The Qur'an was sent down as a single whole from the Preserved Tablet (*al–Lawhal Mahfuz*) on *Laylat al-Qadr* in Ramadan. It was thereupon installed in the House of Glory (*Bait al-Izzat*) in the heaven of the lower world. Then Jibril brought it down and revealed it to the Prophet 🙵 in a series of instalments over a period of twenty-three years."

One year, the Prophet 🙵 summarised the many merits of Ramadan in a *khutbah* delivered on the last day of Sha'ban:

> *"O people! A great and most blessed month comes upon you now, wherein lies a night greater in worth than a thousand months. Fasting during this month is obligatory and extra prayers at night are optional. Whoever draws near to Allah by performing any virtuous deed in this month will have such a reward as if he had performed an obligatory duty at any other time of the year. And whoever performs an obligatory duty shall have the reward of seventy such duties at any other time of the year."*

"This is indeed the month of steadfastness (sabr) and the reward for true steadfastness is the Garden. It is the month of sympathy with one's fellow men. It is a month wherein a believer's livelihood is increased. Whoever feeds a fasting person in order to break the fast at iftar will be forgiven his wrong action and freed from the Fire and he will receive a reward equal to the fasting person, without that person's reward being diminished in the least".

Some of the companions then said, "Not all of us possess the means whereby we can provide enough for a fasting person to break his fast". The Prophet 🌸 replied: "Allah grants the same reward to him who gives a fasting person a single date or a sip of milk or a drink of water to break the fast."

"This is a month the first part of which is mercy, the middle of which is forgiveness and the last part of which is freedom from the Fire. Whosoever lessens the burdens of his servants in this month Allah will forgive him and free him from the Fire. And four things you should endeavour to perform in great number, two of which are to please your Lord while the other two are those you cannot make do without. The first two qualities are to bear witness that there is no god but Allah and to ask for forgiveness. And as for the two you cannot do without: ask Allah for the Garden and seek refuge from the Fire."

"And whoever gives a fasting Muslim water to drink at iftar, Allah will grant him a drink during the Day of Judgement from the fountain of Muhammad after which he shall never again feel thirsty until he enters the Garden".
(Ibn Khuzaymah, narrated by Salman al-Farsi)

It is clear from this *khutbah* that Ramadan is more than just a month of abstention from food and drink during daylight hours. This abstention coupled with acts of sincere *ibadah* helps to redirect the body's energy from the worldly to the divine. Special mention is made in the *khutbah* of the merits of extra prayers at night, *dhikr* and *du'a* and also of feeding a fasting person at *iftar*. Allah has promised to magnify the reward of any good deed in this month, so we should avail ourselves of this unique opportunity and engage in sincere and committed acts of worship, fulfilling both the rights of Allah and of our fellow human beings. This will cultivate self-discipline and generosity, and empathy with the suffering of the poor. Not only is the reward of such a believer increased in the Hereafter but his livelihood is also increased in this world.

It is difficult to exaggerate the bounties of this month but suffice it to say that of the three persons that the Prophet ﷺ cursed, one is the unfortunate Muslim who finds Ramadan in good health but does not use the opportunity to seek Allah's mercy.

2)

THE RULINGS ON FASTING

THE fast of Ramadan is the fourth pillar of Islam and is an obligation upon every responsible Muslim who is capable of doing it. Fasting in Ramadan is an effective form of worship and leads to the moral, spiritual and social development of the individual. It is therefore important to know how to carry this out correctly in order to derive maximum benefit from it.

2.1 People Exempted from Fasting During Ramadan

Fasting during Ramadan is obligatory on every sane adult Muslim, male or female. However, the following groups are exempted:

The insane or mentally deranged.
It is not obligatory for the insane to fast neither is it valid if they do so because they are devoid of sanity which is the basis for performing religious duties.

Children.
Fasting is not obligatory for children before they attain the age of puberty (*balagh*). However, if they choose to fast this is valid and it is good

training for children if parents encourage them to fast. Immediately upon reaching puberty, fasting becomes obligatory.

Seriously ill.

Those who are genuinely ill and fear that fasting will worsen their condition or result in real harm, should not fast. If someone has begun the day fasting but falls seriously ill during the day and fears that continuing the fast will worsen their condition, then they should break the fast. Any fasts that are missed or broken by an ill person should be made up upon recovery at a later date (*qada*).

Chronically ill.

The chronically ill who have little hope of returning to health or who are dependant on medication during daylight hours can substitute their fasts by feeding a needy person. This is called *fidyah* (ransom).

Elderly people.

Elderly people who are weak and unable to fast at any time of the year and who have no prospect of being able to fast are exempt from fasting. However, according to the Hanafi and Shafi'i *madhhabs* they must pay the *fidyah*. In the best known position of the Maliki *madhhab*, it is recommended. If they cannot afford to pay it, they should seek forgiveness from Allah for their shortcomings. The Hanbalis maintain that while the *fidyah* is recommended, it is not obligatory.

Pregnant and nursing mothers.

If a pregnant or a nursing mother fears that fasting may be detrimental to her health or that of her baby, she is permitted to refrain from fasting. Any fasts missed must be made up at a later date when she is capable of it (*qada*). However, there are different views as to whether she should give *fidyah* in addition to making up the missed fasts. In this regard the Hanafis observe that it is not obligatory. The Malikis are of the opinion that it is obligatory for a nursing woman though not for a pregnant one. The Hanbalis and the Shafi'is say that giving the *fidyah* is obligatory upon a pregnant or a nursing woman only if she fears harm for her child, but if she fears harm for her own health as well as that of the child, she is only bound to perform the fasts missed and not required to give the *fidyah*.

Menstruating women/post-natal bleeding.

The fast of a woman in the state of menstruation (*hayd*) or post-natal bleeding (*nifaas*) is not valid. The missed fasts must be made up at a later date (*qada*).

Traveller.

The following conditions should be met for a person to be classified as a traveller:

- ⟩ Distance: The majority opinion is that the journey should be greater than 48 miles from home.
- ⟩ The intention to stay at the place of arrival should be for a period of:
  a) 15 days or less according to Hanafi *fiqh*
  b) 4 days or less according to Maliki and Shafi'i *fiqh*
  c) Less than four days according to Hanbali *fiqh*
  In all cases the day of arrival and the day of departure are not included.
- ⟩ The journey should commence before dawn and the traveller should have reached the point from where the prescribed prayer becomes due before dawn. Hence if someone commences the journey after the dawn, it is unlawful for that person to break the fast, except in the Maliki *madhhab* which permits travellers to break their fast after departure if there is a need.

If the above conditions are fulfilled then it is permissible to forgo the fast and make it up at a later date (*qada*).

Although the concession is granted to forgo the fast for any such journey, even one of 48 miles or more, it is better to consider the effect that the journey will have on the traveller. If fasting during travel will cause genuine hardship then it can be postponed and must be made up at a later date (*qada*). If there is no such constraint then the traveller may fast. However, one must not deliberately make travel plans during Ramadan to avoid fasting.

2.2 The Essentials of Fasting

There are two essentials parts of fasting:
a) *Niyyah* (intention)
b) Refraining from those acts which invalidate the fast.

a) It is essential to make the *niyyah* (intention) to fast. This must be in the heart but it can also be expressed in words according to the Hanafi *madhhab*. An example of an intention is:

وَبِالصَّوْم غَدأ نَـوَيْتُ مِن شَهْر رَمَضَانَ

Wabi saumi ghadin nawaytu min shahri Ramadan
I intend to fast tomorrow in the month of Ramadan.

The intention to fast the following day must be made during any part of the night (from sunset until just before dawn). The intention to fast must be present in the heart each night for the following day's fast to be valid. In the Maliki *madhhab* it is only obligatory to intend the fast at the beginning of the month intending to fast the whole month. However, in that case, someone who travels during the month must on becoming resident again, form the intention to fast the rest of the month. The *niyyah* can be made in a state of ritual impurity.

b) It is essential to refrain from those acts that invalidate the fast beginning from the first light of dawn (*fajr*) and ending when the sun sets (*maghrib*).

2.3 The Etiquettes of Fasting

⟩   It is highly recommended to take the pre-dawn meal (*suhur*). The Prophet ﷺ would wake up early for the night prayer (*tahajjud*), as he ordinarily did, and later eat *suhur*. He urged people to have this meal as it is a mercy and blessing from Allah and makes the fast easier:

> *None of you should miss it even if it is a sip of water since Allah and His angels bless those who have the dawn meal.* (Ahmad)

⟩   The day should be spent engaging in good deeds as the Prophet ﷺ did. His day would be spent in devotion, prayer, *dhikr*, service to others, and teaching and admonishing people. He would pray in the mosque.

⟩   One should refrain from all wrong actions such as lying and backbiting. The Prophet ﷺ said:

> *When any of you is fasting, let him not commit sin…* (Bukhari)

> *Whoever does not stop speaking falsehood and acting in accordance with it, Allah has no need of him giving up his food and drink.* (Bukhari)

⟩ It is recommended to supplicate at the time of *iftar*. The Prophet ﷺ said:

> The fasting person's du'a when he breaks his fast is not rejected. (Ibn Majah)

⟩ The following *du'as* are recommended upon breaking the fast:

اللَّـهُمَّ لَكَ صُمْتُ وَعَلَى رِزْقِكَ أَفْطَرْتُ

Allahumma laka sumtu wa 'ala rizqika aftartu

O Allah, for You I have fasted and on Your provision I break my fast. (Abu Dawud)

ذَهَبَ الظَّمَأُ وَابْتَلَّتِ الْعُرُوقُ وَثَبَتَ
الْأَجْرُ إِنْ شَاءَ اللَّهُ

Dhahaba az-zama', wa'btallat al-'urooq, wa thabat a'l-ajru insha'Allah

Thirst is gone, veins are flowing again, and the reward is certain, *insha'Allah*. (Abu Dawud)

اَللَّـهُمَّ إِنِّي أَسْأَلُكَ بِرَحْمَتِكَ الَّتِي وَسِعَتْ
كُلَّ شَيْءٍ أَنْ تَغْفِرَ لِي

Allahumma inni as'aluka birahmatika al-lati wasi'at kulla shay'in an taghfira li

O Allah, I ask you by Your mercy which envelopes all things, that You forgive me. (Ibn Abi Mulaykah)

⟩ It is highly recommended to hasten the breaking of the fast when the time comes, as the Prophet ﷺ recommended:

> My nation will continue to be well as long as they hasten to break their fast and delay the morning meal. (Ahmad)

⟋ The Prophet ﷺ used to eat dates and drink water to break his fast.
*The Prophet used to break his fast with fresh dates before praying;
if fresh dates were not available, he would eat (dried) dates; if
dried dates were not available, he would have a few sips of water.*
(At-Tirmidhi)

⟋ It is disliked to eat too much, as the Prophet ﷺ said:
*No human ever filled a vessel worse than the stomach. Sufficient for any
son of Adam are some morsels to keep his back straight. But if it must
be, then one third for his food, one third for his drink and one third for
his breath.* (Ahmad, At-Tirmidhi, An-Nasa'i and Ibn Majah)

While this holds true throughout the year, it becomes even more
important during the month of Ramadan.

2.4 Actions that Invalidate the Fast

There are two types of actions that will invalidate the fast: the more
serious actions will necessitate atonement (*kaffarah*) AND restitution
(*qada*), while the less serious actions will require restitution only, i.e.
that fast must be made up at a later date (*qada*).

Ibn Juzayy says about restitution (*qada*): "Whoever deliberately breaks
an obligatory fast must make up for it, as must those who break the fast
with some permissible excuse such as illness and travel. And someone
who breaks a fast out of forgetfulness must make up for it [according
to the Maliki school] but contrary to [Imam ash-Shafi'i and Imam Abu
Hanifah]."

Ibn Juzayy says about atonement (*kaffarah*): "The reason for [performing
kaffarah] is because of having deliberately ruined a fast of Ramadan in

particular, intending to rend the sanctity of the fast without any reason which would render breaking the fast permissible."

Actions that necessitate atonement (*kaffarah*) AND restitution (*qada*)

Deliberate eating/drinking/smoking/chewing gum.
If someone engages in these acts deliberately and voluntarily while knowing they are fasting, and without a valid reason, the fast becomes invalid and necessitates both *kaffarah* and *qada*.

Deliberate ingestion of other materials or alternative forms of nourishment.
This includes: **a)** deliberately passing anything down the gullet that is not usually used as food, in which case there are differences of opinion as to whether *kaffarah* is obligatory; or **b)** deliberately taking nourishment through other means such as glucose injections. In this case, only Hanafi *fiqh* stipulates that *kaffarah* is necessary in addition to *qada*. The Hanbali, Maliki and Shafi'i position is that such an act necessitates *qada* only.

Deliberate sexual intercourse.
Deliberately engaging in sexual intercourse during daylight hours invalidates the fast and necessitates both *qada* and *kaffarah*.

Deliberate ejaculation of sperm.
This will invalidate the fast whether it is caused by kissing/caressing one's wife or is self-induced whether by looking at or thinking about what will cause sexual arousal [or by masturbation] and continuing to do that until ejaculation. This necessitates both *kaffarah* and *qada* according to the Maliki and Hanbali schools, but *qada* only according to the Shafi'i and Hanafi schools.

Actions that necessitate restitution (*qada*) only

Accidentally eating/drinking/smoking/chewing gum.
Accidentally engaging in these activities while fasting necessitates *qada* only according to the Hanbali and Maliki *madhahib*. This includes nourishment accidentally provided by means other than oral, for example glucose injections.

Accidental sexual intercourse.
If one engages in sexual intercourse by accident or forgetting that one is fasting, then according to the Maliki and Hanbali schools only, it necessitates *qada* but not *kaffarah*.

Pre-ejaculatory fluid.
In the Maliki and Hanbali schools, but not the Hanafi or Shafi'i schools, if a man kisses, or caresses or embraces his wife until he is aroused and emits pre-ejaculatory fluid, then he must make *qada* for that fast. If he experiences arousal without the emission of pre-ejaculatory fluid, then *qada* is not necessary.

Deliberate vomiting.
Deliberately inducing vomiting will invalidate the fast regardless of whether the vomited amount is large or small. The person must make *qada*. There is a difference of opinion in the Maliki school as to whether such an act necessitates *kaffarah* as well.

Menstrual bleeding or post–natal bleeding.
If either of these two types of bleeding start at any time between *salat al-Fajr* and *salat al-Maghrib*, then the whole fast is invalid and must be made up later (*qada*).

Making the intention to stop fasting.

According to the Hanbali *madhhab*, this will invalidate the fast necessitating *qada*, even if the person has not acted on the intention, since one of the pre-requisites of fasting is the *niyyah*.

Nose drops.

Inserting drops of medicine or water through the nose will invalidate the fast since the nose is a passage to the stomach, and will necessitate *qada*.

2.5 Acts that do not Invalidate the Fast

Accidentally eating/drinking/smoking/chewing gum.

If someone accidentally engages in one of these acts in a moment of forgetfulness of the fasting state, then this will not invalidate the fast provided that the act is stopped once the faster realises his error, according to the Hanafi and Shafi'i schools, on the basis of the following hadith narrated by Abu Huraira 🕉 that the Prophet 🕌 said:

> *Whoever forgets - while fasting - and eats or drinks, should stop immediately and resume or complete his fast, for he has just been fed and quenched by Allah.* (Agreed Upon)

However, according to the Maliki and Hanbali *madhahib* the person must make *qada* for it.

Accidental sexual intercourse.

If this act has been committed in a moment of forgetfulness, then the fast will remain valid only according to the Hanafi and Shafi'i *madhahib* (but not the Maliki and Hanafi *madhahib* which impose a *qada*).

Involuntary vomiting.
This does not invalidate the fast regardless of the quantity expelled.

Nose bleed.

Involuntary daytime ejaculation.
There is neither *qada* nor *kaffarah* required for involuntary ejaculation during the daytime such as a wet-dream while asleep.

Involuntary swallowing.
Involuntary swallowing of saliva or dust or minute particles does not invalidate the fast. If one swallows saliva containing food particles (less than the size of a grain of gram) stuck between the teeth this does not nullify the fast if this was not deliberate. However, it is best to rinse the mouth and brush the teeth thoroughly after *suhur*.

Rinsing the mouth and nose.
This is permissible as it is part of *wudu*. Care should be taken that the water does not reach the back of the mouth or go too far up the nose. Laqit ibn Sabra reported that the Prophet ﷺ said:

> *Exaggerate when rinsing your nose unless you are fasting.* (An-Nasa'i, Abu Dawud, At-Tirmidhi and Ibn Majah)

Injections.
These do not invalidate the fast regardless of whether they are intravenous, muscular or subcutaneous as long as they **do not provide nourishment.** Therefore, vaccinations do not invalidate the fast.

Giving blood.
This is allowed as long as it does not weaken the donor. Thabit al-Bunani asked Anas ﷺ:

> 'Did you dislike cupping for a fasting person during the time of the
> Prophet?' He answered: 'No (we did not), unless it made someone weak.'
> (Bukhari)

And it was customary in cupping to let some blood. For this reason
having a blood test would also not invalidate the fast.

Swallowing mucus or phlegm.

Brushing teeth without toothpaste or using a miswak.
Amir bin Rabeelah narrated:

> I saw the Messenger of Allah ﷺ on numerous occasions chewing siwaak
> while fasting. (At-Tirmidhi)

Some caution should be exercised in the use of toothpaste. If any
portion of it is swallowed then the fast is invalidated. Furthermore, the
use of toothpaste necessitates thorough and exaggerated rinsing out of
the mouth to expel it completely, so it is recommended that if one does
brush the teeth with toothpaste it is done before *fajr* time after *suhur*.

Kissing your spouse.
This is allowed as long as one remains in complete control of his actions
and can be sure that this will not lead to seminal ejection. In the Maliki
school it is disapproved for someone in control of his sexual appetite to
embrace or kiss, but for someone who has little control of it, it is *haram*.
It is confirmed that A'ishah ﷺ said:

> The Prophet ﷺ would kiss and embrace while he was fasting, for he had the
> most control of all of you over his desires. (Bukhari and Muslim)

To pour water on the head and face.
Abu Bakr ibn Abd ar-Rahman ﷺ reported from a number of
companions that they had seen Allah's Messenger ﷺ pour water over

his head while he was fasting due to thirst or extreme heat. (Ahmad, Malik, and Abu Dawud)

Eye drops.
The use of eye drops for medicinal purposes is permitted on the strength of the following hadith:

> *Al-A'mash said, 'I never saw any of our companions disliking the application of kohl for the one fasting.' Ibrahim (An-Nakha'i) would allow the one fasting to apply aloes to his eyes.* (Abu Dawud)

Eye drops do not invalidate the fast even if the taste reaches the back of the throat. This is because the eyes are not a regular passage for food or nourishment. In the Maliki school there are differences of opinion, one of which is that the case of kohl depends on whether it dissolves or not. If it dissolves and thus reaches the throat, it breaks the fast.

Ear drops, ear syringing, oiling the ears.
According to the Hanbali and Hanafi *madhahib*, these acts do not invalidate fasting even if the taste is felt at the back of the throat. However, the ears are considered an open passage according to the Shafi'i *madhhab*, therefore these acts would necessitate *qada* from the Shafi'i position. According to the Malikis if anything reaches the back of the throat through the three passages of the mouth, the nose and the ears, the fast has been broken, thus necessitating *qada*.

Asthma inhaler.
The use of such medication does not invalidate the fast since it will neither provide nourishment nor reach the stomach but is intended to reach the lungs.

Vaginal bleeding.

Vaginal bleeding that is neither menstruation (*hayd*) nor post-natal bleeding (*nifaas*), e.g., bleeding during pregnancy or beyond the normal time of *hayd* or *nifaas* will not invalidate the fast.

Tasting food.

This is permitted only if absolutely necessary and only with the tip of the tongue so that the food does not reach the back of the mouth. A situation in which this might be acceptable is if a woman needs to check that the food she has prepared is not spoiled.

2.6 Qada (Restitution)

$$\text{فَعِدَّةٌ مِّنْ أَيَّامٍ أُخَرَ}$$

The prescribed number (should be made up) from days later. (2:185)

Qada becomes necessary either when someone has forgone a fast completely or has broken it with an action that necessitates *qada* as described previously. These fasts should ideally be kept as soon as possible after Ramadan, without delay unless there is a good reason. There is one *qada* fast for every one missed fast of Ramadan. If there are many *qada* fasts to be kept, one has a choice of fasting on consecutive days or on random days throughout the year. The fasts can be made up on any day except those days on which it is prohibited to fast (the two 'Eid days and the days of *Tashreeq* i.e. the three days following 'Eid al-Adha).

It is necessary to make the *niyyah* for the *qada* fast before the time of *fajr* (as with a Ramadan fast) although it is not necessary to specify which day it is restitution for. If the *niyyah* has not been made by *salat al-Fajr*, then the fast becomes a *nafl* fast and the *qada* fast will need to be repeated.

If a person has not kept the *qada* fasts of Ramadan and the following Ramadan commences without his having made the *qada*, he should keep the fasts of the present Ramadan and make up the *qada* fasts of the previous Ramadan after *'Eid*. However, this is a highly undesirable practice without good reason. According to the Malikis, Shafi'is and Hanbalis, a person is also due to pay the *fidyah* ransom of a *mudd* of food per day at the time he or she makes up the fast.

2.7 *Fidyah* (Ransom)

Fidyah is the compensation which has to be paid for those fasts which have been missed by the following groups:
) Elderly depending on the *madhhab* followed
) Chronically ill
) Pregnant/nursing mothers depending on the *madhhab* followed

These people are obliged to feed one poor person (*miskin*) a day for every day of fasting that they do not perform. *Fidyah* can only be given to those who can accept *zakat*. There is some difference amongst scholars as to how much food is to be supplied to the needy since this has not been stipulated in hadith. There are several options as to how this can be given.

) The amount of staple (wheat, grain, rice) can be given directly to the needy either on a daily basis or the whole amount due at one time. It can be given to several people or to one or two families.
) A prepared meal can be given to the needy either individually daily

or one meal can be used to feed as many people as fasts that need to be compensated. Anas bin Malik, at an advanced age, fed poor people bread and meat one or two days every year (Bukhari).

) Some scholars permit money to be given in lieu of food to a charitable organisation/individual who will purchase the relevant amount of food to feed the needy with.

If someone dies without having paid outstanding *fidyah*, then this must be done by his relatives from the wealth of the deceased.

2.8 *Kaffarah* (Atonement)

The atonement for intentionally breaking the fast in Ramadan is:
) The freeing of a slave
) Fasting for two consecutive months
) Feeding sixty poor persons

The Malikis allow an option between any one of these. That is, a sane adult may choose between freeing a slave, fasting or feeding the poor, except that in the majority opinion the best is to feed the poor. The Shafi'is, Hanbalis and Hanafis impose atonement in the aforementioned order. That is, releasing a slave is specifically obligatory, and only if this is not possible does fasting become obligatory and so on.

If a person is unable to offer any form of atonement, he will remain liable for it until he comes to possess the capacity to offer it according to the Shafi'i, Maliki and Hanafi positions. However, the Hanbalis are of the opinion that if one is unable to offer *kaffarah*, the obligation is lifted, even if that person is later able to atone.

It is not permissible for someone on whom fasting for two consecutive months has become obligatory, to miss even a single fast during these two months, because that would break their continuity. Hence, on the missing of a fast the person should fast anew for two months.

The number of atonements should be equal to the number of forbidden acts that caused it, so that a person who breaks two fasts will have to give two atonements. But someone who breaks one fast several times in the same day is liable for only one atonement.

3)

THE ESSENCE OF FASTING

يَٰٓأَيُّهَا ٱلَّذِينَ ءَامَنُوا كُتِبَ عَلَيۡكُمُ ٱلصِّيَامُ
كَمَا كُتِبَ عَلَى ٱلَّذِينَ مِن قَبۡلِكُمۡ لَعَلَّكُمۡ تَنَّقُونَ

**You who have *iman*! Fasting is prescribed for you, as it was
prescribed for those before you – so that hopefully you will
have *taqwa*. (2:183)**

FASTING has been prescribed for us by Allah in order to make us
people of *taqwa*. But what is *taqwa*?

Taqwa is that people do not find a fault in your speech and the
angels do not find a fault in your actions whilst the angels of the
throne see no fault in your inner motives. *(Ibrahim ibn Adham)*

In order to reach this stage, we must develop a high level of consciousness
of Allah; be eager to please Him and fearful of disobeying Him. Earning
the pleasure of Allah can be achieved by passing through several grades
or degrees of *taqwa*[1]:

---

1. See Ibn Juzayy's *Kitab at-tashil fi 'ulum at-tanzil*, his tafsir of the Qur'an.

⌐ that the slave should protect himself from *kufr* (covering over the truth), and that is the station of Islam;

⌐ that he should protect himself from acts of disobedience and forbidden things, and this is the station of turning to Allah or repentance (*tawbah*);

⌐ that he should protect himself from doubtful matters, and that is the station of caution or scrupulousness (*wara'*);

⌐ that he should protect himself from even those things that are permitted, and that is the station of doing without (*zuhd*);

⌐ that he should protect himself from the presence of other than Allah in his heart, and that is the station of witnessing (*mushahadah*).

The reward for those who have attained *taqwa*, the *mutaqeen*, is the Garden. Therefore, fasting is a means to attain the highest honour in the Eternal Life, which is what all Muslims strive for. So how does fasting help us to achieve this? In a hadith, the Prophet ﷺ stated:

Shaytan flows in the son of Adam with the flowing of the blood. (Bukhari and Muslim)

To that some of the people of knowledge added:

so tighten his passages with hunger. (See Kashf al-Khafa)

Regardless of our circumstances, we are constrained by physical needs for our well being; the need for food, drink, mental rest, company and leisure. For many of us the fulfilment of these needs is the focus of our entire lives. We work in order to earn money so as to satisfy these needs. The more we earn, the more we consume, thus necessitating the need to earn more. This vicious cycle is a hallmark of this modern consumer society that distracts our attention away from spirituality.

Fasting is the perfect antidote to this excessive lifestyle. It is through fasting that we can move away from the physical and material world and towards the spiritual world. By fasting, by controlling food and drink intake, regulating speech and sleep and experiencing the spiritual realm we temporarily become relatively free of our physical needs, thus escaping for a while the prison of the senses.

The obsessive quest to fulfil physical needs is a veil between man and his Creator, which fasting lifts. Whilst fasting, there is the sense of closeness to Allah, peace of mind, a feeling of freedom and a state of relaxation and tranquillity. Fasting restrains carnal desire and those cravings which, if left uncontrolled, would weaken the soul and eventually destroy it. In fact, the whole month of Ramadan is a programme that enables us to become acquainted with the spiritual world and to nourish the soul rather than the body.

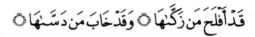

He who purifies it [the self] has succeeded, he who covers it up has failed. (91:9–10)

But the benefits of fasting are not only confined to the Hereafter. There are also great personal and social benefits. Allah has given us the qualities of self-restraint and self-discipline which prevent us from caving into our desires whenever we feel. However, we are surrounded by temptations that erode our level of self-control and allow us to succumb to our desires easily. It is at this point that our desires begin to control us and we become vulnerable and exposed to them. But in a *hadith qudsi*, we are told that fasting is a shield for the believer. It will protect us; it will give us the strength to gain mastery over our desires; it will make us people of strong and noble moral character.

Noble moral character is expressed through such qualities as honesty, respect for others, sacrifice, generosity, patience and abandonment of those traits that are governed by our base desires. A society made up of upstanding people who care for and respect each other is a strong and healthy one, while a society that gives in to its desires is a selfish one.

Fasting is an effective means of developing character, because it teaches the principle of self-denial therefore encouraging sacrifice for others. It is about becoming more aware of others, their rights and our responsibilities. It makes us more charitable and giving, with genuine concern and sincerity rather than a sense of duty. How many of us can empathise with a hungry man when our bellies are overfull?

> Whoever eats little will understand and make others understand and will be clear and humble. Overeating weighs a person down and keeps him from much of what he wants (to accomplish). *(Muhammad ibn Wasi)*

Fasting in Ramadan also fosters a sense of community and equality as young and old, rich and poor, employee and employer all observe the same practices. This creates an atmosphere of unity, because everyone is doing the same thing: fasting, praying and reciting the Qur'an. There is a sense of brotherhood and sisterhood, a sense of belonging to a community of believers in which one is valued.

There are numerous health benefits from a fast conducted properly, although these are considered secondary to those benefits outlined above. Abu Huraira narrated that the Prophet ﷺ said:

> *Fast and you will attain good health.* (Ibn as-Sunni and Abu Nu'aym)

Abstention from food and drink allows the gastro-intestinal system to rest and rehabilitate thus encouraging healing of the body. It allows the body time to flush out toxic matter that has built up over the months and actually revives and rejuvenates the millions of cells in the body. It improves circulation, stamina and strength as well as lowering cholesterol, blood sugar and systolic blood pressure. All these medical benefits have been well-documented in the literature.

In order to reap all these benefits from fasting, we must not treat it as merely an exercise in abstaining from food and drink for a few hours. It is complete abstinence from all bad habits, without which fasting is rendered invalid.

Whoever does not give up lying and cheating, Allah has no need of him giving up eating and drinking. (Muslim)

In order to derive full benefit from the fast, it is important to take care that each of our body parts does not engage in any *haram* act. The eyes must be controlled so that they do not see inappropriate images; the tongue should not engage in gossip, lying or backbiting or even utter words that could hurt someone's feelings; the ears should not listen to any inappropriate speech whether gossip and backbiting, or through music and TV; the feet must not walk towards a place where *haram* acts are taking place.

The blessing of the fast can only be obtained if the food with which the fast is broken is *halal* and pure and obtained through *halal* means. And even where the food is *halal* and obtained by *halal* means, it is not the right time to indulge in a great deal of food, or in luxurious types of food. It is a privilege from Allah that we are able to enjoy His bounties at *suhur* and *iftar* times and we must be careful not to defeat the purpose of the fast by eating to excess foods that are rarely seen at other times of the year.

We must fast with humility and be anxious to gain the pleasure of Allah through our acts of *ibadah*, acts which should continue in the night, to the extent that we are able, with the same fervour as during the day.

4

SALAT AT-TARAWIH AND QUR'AN

Origin of Tarawih

It is narrated by A'ishah ☺: "The Prophet ☺ offered salah [at-Tarawih] in the mosque and many people prayed with him. The next day he did the same and more people prayed with him. Then the people gathered on the third night but the Prophet ☺ did not come out to them. In the morning, he said to them, 'Surely I saw what you did, and nothing prevented me from coming out to you, save that I feared that [that prayer] would be made obligatory upon you.' And that was during Ramadan." (Bukhari and Muslim)

It was during the Caliphate of 'Umar ibn al-Khattab ☺ that *salat at-Tarawih* was performed as a congregational prayer behind one *imam*. Abd ar-Rahman ibn Abdulqari reports:

"One night during Ramadan, I went with 'Umar ☺ to the mosque and the people were praying in different groups. Some were praying by themselves and others were praying in small groups. 'Umar ☺ said: 'I think it would be better if I gathered them under one imam.' Then he did so and appointed Ubayy ibn Ka'b as the leader of the prayer. Then I went out with him on another night and all the people were praying behind one imam and 'Umar ☺ said: 'What a good innovation (bid'ah) this is,' but, it is better to sleep

and delay it until the latter portion of the night.' The people (however) prayed it at the beginning of the night." (Bukhari, Ibn Khuzaymah and Al-Bayhaqi)

How to Perform Tarawih

Tarawih are supererogatory prayers: they are strongly recommended and are *sunnah mu'akkadah*, but not *wajib*. Regarding the number of *rak'at*, there is a difference of opinion as to whether there are eight, twenty or thirty-six. Traditionally, Muslims everywhere have offered twenty. This is inherited from the practice of 'Umar ﷺ, during whose time there was no dispute on this issue.

> *In the time of 'Umar ibn al-Khattab ﷺ the people used to observe twenty rak'at and the witr.* (Al-Bayhaqi in Ma'rifat as-sunan wa'l athar)

> *The Prophet ﷺ said, "Follow my Sunnah and the Sunnah of the rightly-guided khulafa after me."*

There are also some reports of thirty-six *rak'at* of *tarawih* according to Imam Malik.

> *Ibn al-Qasim said, "The rak'at (of tarawih) with witr are thirty-nine."* *Imam Malik said, "This is what the people have agreed upon from amongst the predecessors, and the people have not stopped doing it."*

The practice of thirty-six *rak'at* was that of the people of Madinah at the time of 'Umar ibn Abdul Aziz and Imam Malik ibn Anas ﷺ. The number of *rak'at* of *tarawih* prayed in congregation were twenty and the people of Madinah used to perform an extra four *rak'at* without congregation during the rest periods after every four *rak'at* of congregational *tarawih*. This amounted to an extra sixteen *rak'at* in addition to the congregational twenty *rak'at*. The reason that the Madinans introduced the extra prayers was because the people of Makkah would perform *tawaf* around the Ka'bah after every four *rak'at* of congregational *tarawih*, and these extra prayers were a form of compensation.

Today twenty *rak'at* of *tarawih* are performed in both *al-Masjid al-Haram* in Makkah and *al-Masjid an-Nabawi* in Madinah. The schools also concur that *salat at-Tarawih* consists of twenty *rak'at*, except that this is the less well known position in the Maliki school who still recommend thirty-six *rak'at*.

Imam Ali al-Qari al-Hanafi said in Sharh an-Nuqayah:

> *Imam al-Bayhaqi has reported on genuine authority (sahih) about the performance of twenty rak'ahs of Tarawih during the periods of 'Umar, 'Uthman and 'Ali* 🌼, *and hence there has been consensus (ijma') on it.*

Salat at-Tarawih can be performed after *salat al-'Isha* and before *salat al-Fajr*. It can be done individually or in congregation although there is great reward in attending congregation. It is performed in sets of two *rak'at* and there is a rest period after every four *rak'at*. It is recommended to wait for a period (equal to four *rak'at* of prayer) after each four *rak'at* that are offered and between the fifth interval and the *witr* prayer. This was the practice of the right-acting predecessors since Ubayy ibn Ka'b led the Muslims in the *tarawih* prayer. Abu Hanifah stated that this is inferred from the Arabic word *tarawih* (from the Arabic root *rawwaha* meaning 'to have a rest'). There are no hadith indicating what should be said or done in these intervals, although one can do *dhikr*, make *du'a* or remain silent.

The three *rak'at* of witr can be said after the *tarawih* is complete, although if one chooses then to pray *tahajjud*, one can offer the *witr* after *salat at-Tahajjud*.

The *tarawih* prayer precedes the fast so that upon breaking the last fast according to some there will be no *tarawih* prayers that night, but again some others observe *tarawih* on this last night too.

It is highly meritorious to read the Qur'an in its entirety once in Ramadan as the Prophet ﷺ used to recite the entire content of the Qur'an that had been revealed up to that time to Jibril every Ramadan. In the year of his death, he read the entire Qur'an twice in Ramadan to Jibril. It is narrated that he ﷺ said:

> *Fasting and the Qur'an intercede for a man. Fasting says, "O my Lord, I have kept him away from his food and his passions by day, so accept my intercession for him." The Qur'an says, "I have kept him away from sleep by night, so accept my intercession for him." Then their intercession is accepted.* (Al-Bayhaqi)

It is also acceptable, rather than reciting the Qur'an oneself, to listen to the entire contents of the Qur'an being read out in *tarawih* prayers throughout Ramadan. Indeed, the *'ulama* say that listening to the Qur'an attentively when it is recited in one's presence is obligatory because Allah said:

وَإِذَا قُرِئَ ٱلْقُرْءَانُ فَٱسْتَمِعُوا۟ لَهُۥ وَأَنصِتُوا۟ لَعَلَّكُمْ تُرْحَمُونَ

When the Qur'an is recited listen to it and be quiet so that hopefully you will gain mercy. (7:204)

On the other hand, reciting the Qur'an is a *sunnah* and is not obligatory, and obligations take precedence over *sunnan*.

'Umar ﷺ ordered me (Ubayy) to lead the people in prayer at night in Ramadan, because the people fast during the day and can not recite (the Qur'an) well, therefore it is better that you should recite (the Qur'an) during the night. I (Ubayy) asked: "Commander of the believers, this thing was not done before." He said: "I know, but it is a good practice", and so I (Ubayy) led (the Companions) in twenty rak'at."

5)

THE LAST TEN DAYS OF RAMADAN

It was reported by A'ishah ﷠ that "The Prophet ﷺ would strive to do good deeds during the last ten days of Ramadan more than at any other time of the year." (Muslim)

The last ten days of Ramadan bring freedom from the Fire of Hell according to the Prophet's ﷺ Ramadan *khutbah* quoted earlier in the book. It is an opportunity for us to increase in our *ibadah* to avail ourselves of the last precious days of Ramadan, which also contain the most important night: *Laylat al-Qadr*.

Laylat al-Qadr

One of the special features of Ramadan is *Laylat al-Qadr*, the Night of Power. It is the best of all the nights in the year as the following surah explains:

إِنَّا أَنزَلْنَهُ فِى لَيْلَةِ ٱلْقَدْرِ ۝

وَمَآ أَدْرَىٰكَ مَا لَيْلَةُ ٱلْقَدْرِ ۝

لَيْلَةُ ٱلْقَدْرِ خَيْرٌ مِّنْ أَلْفِ شَهْرٍ ۝

تَنَزَّلُ ٱلْمَلَـٰٓئِكَةُ وَٱلرُّوحُ فِيهَا بِإِذْنِ رَبِّهِم مِّن كُلِّ أَمْرٍ ۝

سَلَـٰمٌ هِىَ حَتَّىٰ مَطْلَعِ ٱلْفَجْرِ ۝

Truly We sent it down on the Night of Power.
And what will convey to you what the Night of Power is?
The Night of Power is better than a thousand months.

In it the angels and the Ruh descend by their Lord's authority
with every ordinance.

It is Peace – until the coming of the dawn.
(Surah 97)

This was the night chosen by Allah for the revelation of His Divine Word to mankind. This was the night in which mankind was gifted with the Key to Success in this world and the Next, a light to guide us for all time. This was the night in which we were given the means to achieve peace and harmony both within ourselves and among ourselves. If we begin to consider the consequences of the events of that night, we see that they have had a more far-reaching effect than we can imagine.

And what will convey to you what the Night of Power is?

This night is better than a thousand months, and as people have pointed out, a thousand months is longer than the average lifespan. So this is a night that is better than an entire life. Many thousands of months, indeed years, have passed without producing a comparable event that resulted in changes like those brought about as a consequence of the events of that night.

We should spend the night in sincere devotion and *ibadah* seeking the pleasure of Allah. Allah has sent down angels, the purest of creatures, to pray with us and for us and to grace us with their presence if we choose to avail ourselves of this opportunity.

As an *ummah*, we tend to underestimate the value and importance of this night. After all, if we were asked by our employer to work through the night for financial gain, we would endeavour to please them in order to gain promotion in this life. Yet we overlook the fact that our Creator has offered us forgiveness, peace and elevation to the highest ranks for a night of pure *ibadah* and yet we sleep! Perhaps we have become used to material and immediate rewards, and so matters of spirit may be too esoteric for us to be concerned with.

Anas ﷺ said, "The month of Ramadan began and the Messenger ﷺ said, 'This month has come to you and in it there is a night which is better than a thousand months. Whoever is forbidden it has been forbidden all good, and no one is forbidden its good except for someone who is deprived."
(Ibn Majah)

The Messenger ﷺ said:
Search for Laylat al-Qadr in the odd nights of the last ten days of Ramadan.
(Bukhari)

According to this hadith *Laylat al-Qadr* could fall on the 21st, 23rd, 25th, 27th or 29th nights of Ramadan. (It is important to remember that the night of the 21st, for example, will precede the fast of the 21st day). The exact date of the Night of Power is known only to Allah and there are reasons for keeping the exact date a secret. It is a means of separating the fervent worshippers from those who are less devoted. Those who are keen to earn the blessings of this night and are aware of its splendour will perform *ibadah* on each of the possible dates, while those less devoted will do so on one night only.

There are many ways to perform *ibadah* on this night in order to earn the pleasure of Allah. One can perform *nafl salah* as well as *sunnah salah* such as *salat at-Tahajjud*. While not performing *salah*, one can make *dhikr* or read the Qur'an or make sincere and humble *du'a*. A'ishah ﷺ asked the Messenger ﷺ, "What should I pray on *Laylat al-Qadr*?" He replied, "Pray like this:

اَللَّهُمَّ إِنَّكَ عَفُوٌّ تُحِبُّ الْعَفْوَ ، فَاعْفُ عَنِّي

'Allahumma innaka 'afuwwun tuhibbu'l-'afwa f'afu 'anni'
O Allah, You indeed are pardoning and You love to pardon, so pardon me." (Ahmad)

Abu Huraira 🕮 narrated that the Messenger of Allah 🕮 said:
Whoever stands the night [in prayer] on the Night of the Decree with faith, and seeking rewards [from Allah], his previous wrong actions will be forgiven. (Bukhari and Muslim)

I'tikaf

There are three different types of *i'tikaf*.

Obligatory (*wajib*).

This is when a person takes an oath or makes a pledge that he will go into retreat for a specified number of days, for example, on acceptance of a particular *du'a*. If Allah fulfils his pledge, he must then go into retreat.

'Umar 🕮 *said to the Messenger of Allah 🕮, "Messenger of Allah, I had made a vow to stay one night in the inviolable mosque (as i'tikaf), and the Prophet 🕮 said to him, 'Fulfil your vow.'"* (Ibn Abi 'Asim in al-I'tikaf)

Desirable.

This is whenever a person enters the mosque and makes the intention of a short retreat. According to the Malikis and others, it should be at the least for a night and a day, but according to some schools it can be for even less than a day or for as long as one remains in the mosque.

Sunnah.

This is the highly recommended *i'tikaf* of the last ten days of Ramadan. It is a sunnah that at least one person in a locality goes into retreat.

Narrated A'ishah 🕮 that, "The Prophet 🕮 used to practice i'tikaf in the last ten days of Ramadan until he died and then his wives used to practice i'tikaf after him." (Bukhari)

The Prophet ﷺ would retire to the mosque during the last ten days of Ramadan to temporarily disassociate himself from worldly affairs and to immerse himself totally in the remembrance of Allah. This seclusion, known as *i'tikaf*, is still practised by many Muslims.

The noun *i'tikaf* is derived from the Arabic verb *i'takafa* which means to isolate oneself, to devote oneself diligently to a task and to go into retreat. According to the *shari'ah*, it means to stay in a mosque with the intention of worshipping Allah and drawing closer to Him. *I'tikaf* can be performed in any mosque in which the daily *salah* are held in congregation but if it is done over a period in which *Jumu'ah* occurs then it must be done in a *Jumu'ah* mosque, since if the *Jumu'ah* occurred during the *i'tikaf* the person who was not in a *Jumu'ah* mosque would have to leave it to attend *Jumu'ah* and this would invalidate his *i'tikaf*. But about this, Abu Hanifah had a different view allowing that. In the Hanafi school, women do *i'tikaf* at home, where they can retreat by staying in one room or the corner of a room reserved for prayer. In the other schools of *fiqh*, they do *i'tikaf* in the mosque as the wives of the Prophet ﷺ used to do.

Retreat is an effective means for spiritual development since the devotee temporarily dissociates himself from worldly affairs, spending his day and night immersed in the remembrance of Allah, constantly praying, supplicating, reciting the Glorious Qur'an and meditating. He longs for and yearns to be near his Lord. This highly charged spiritual state of the devotee is graphically captured in *Zad al-Ma'ad*:

> *"The heart becomes attached to Allah, exalted is He, and one attains inner composure and equanimity. Preoccupation with the mundane things of life ceases and absorption in the eternal reality takes its place, and the state is reached in which all fears, hopes and apprehensions are superseded by anxiety for Him and every thought and feeling is blended with the eagerness*

to gain His nearness. Devotion to the Almighty is inculcated instead of devotion to the world and thus it becomes the provision for the grave in which there will be neither friend nor helper. This is the lofty purpose of i'tikaf". (Zad al-Ma'ad)

The Messenger of Allah ﷺ described two benefits of retreat. He said about the person in *i'tikaf*:

He is protected from committing wrong actions and he gets the rewards of good deeds like someone who does all of them. (Ibn Majah)

The first benefit of spiritual retreat is that by being secluded all day and night in the clean environment of the mosque, one has no opportunity to do wrong. Secondly, one is rewarded as if one had done deeds one is unable to perform, like visiting the sick, attending funerals, and serving parents and family. So not only is reward incurred for those good deeds done but also for those not done.

Conditions of I'tikaf

) Fasting is a prerequisite for *i'tikaf* in Ramadan but not for any of the other types, except in the Maliki *madhhab* in which it is a prerequisite.

) Women must be free from menstrual or post-natal bleeding in order to sit in *i'tikaf*. If the menstruation occurs while in *i'tikaf* they come out of it until it is over, when, if possible, they can return.

) Before sitting in *i'tikaf* in Ramadan, it is important to make the intention to do so. This must be made before the sunset of the 19th day. *I'tikaf* will end on the sunset of the last day of Ramadan even though only nine days may have elapsed, but in the Maliki school one remains in *i'tikaf* until it is time to go to the *'Eid* prayer.

It is permissible to leave the mosque during *i'tikaf* for the following reasons:

) To attend the call of nature, do *wudu* or *ghusl*.

) To go to a *jami'ah* mosque for *salat al-Jumu'ah* if it is not held in the same mosque according to the Hanifi school but not the other schools, which consider that the *i'tikaf* should in that case only be held in a *jami'ah* mosque.

) If there is fear or danger of the mosque collapsing, one can leave the mosque to go to another mosque.

) To obtain food if there is no other means to do so.

The following things nullify *i'tikaf*:

) Leaving the mosque: if one is doing obligatory or sunnah *i'tikaf* one cannot leave the mosque except for the legitimate reasons given above. However, if one is doing a voluntary *i'tikaf* then it is permissible to leave the mosque whenever one likes because there is no set limit on how long one is staying in the mosque, except in the Maliki school which considers the least period to be a night and a day.

) Sexual intercourse, intentionally or unintentionally, even without ejaculation, as mentioned in the Qur'an (2:187)
Other sexual activities that cause arousal are absolutely forbidden during it but nevertheless do not nullify *i'tikaf* according to the Hanafi *madhhab* but contrary to the others.

) Becoming unconscious or insane nullifies *i'tikaf*

) Intoxication

) Apostasy

) Being detained because of a debt

) Becoming involved in a major wrong action such as slandering a Muslim's sexual virtue, but about this there is a difference of opinion.

)   Menstruation or bleeding after giving birth for women according to the Hanafi school. According to the Malikis the menstruating woman is under the rule of the *i'tikaf* until the end of her menstruation when, if possible, she returns to *i'tikaf*.

Undesirable Things in I'tikaf

)   Silence becomes undesirable if one believes that it is an act of worship in itself. But if one does not think that, but remains silent because he is absorbed in *dhikr* and meditation then silence is not undesirable. In fact controlling the tongue and keeping quiet can be good actions.

)   Bringing merchandise into the mosque for sale is unacceptable at any time. However, according to a very few of the *'ulama* it is permissible to make a contract of sale in the mosque, but making other kinds of business agreements is not permissible.

It is important at this point to differentiate between worldly pleasures, from which *i'tikaf* offers a retreat, and worldly responsibilities. One must ensure before entering *i'tikaf* that for its duration all dependants are well-provided for and that arrangements are made for their well-being.

The final ten days of Ramadan are a time to earn great blessings and reward if we wish. While some in every community will sit in *i'tikaf*, others should do as much as they are able to make the fullest use of this unique time.

6

THE END OF
RAMADAN

Donations at the end of Ramadan: Sadaqat al-Fitr

FITR means breaking the fast, and *Sadaqat al-Fitr* is the charity given
away at the end of Ramadan. It was enjoined upon all Muslims by the
Prophet ﷺ the same year that fasting was made obligatory.

The payment of *Sadaqat al-Fitr* is obligatory on every Muslim, male or
female, child or adult, who is able to afford it on that day. The Prophet
ﷺ has said:

> Certainly, Sadaqat al-Fitr is a duty incumbent on every Muslim, whether
> male or female, free or slave, minor or major. (At-Tirmidhi)

The *sadaqah* of a slave is paid by his master and the *sadaqah* of a wife is
paid by her husband except according to Abu Hanifah, and the *sadaqah*
of children and the insane is paid by the parents or guardian. According
to the Hanafi *madhhab*, *sadaqah* becomes obligatory on every Muslim
who is alive at the appearance of dawn on the 'Eid day. Thus there is no
sadaqah on a person who dies before dawn or is deprived of wealth and
is reduced to poverty before dawn. Similarly *sadaqah* will be obligatory
for a baby who is born before dawn during the night but not for a baby
who is born afterwards. *Sadaqah* is also obligatory on a person who

embraces Islam before dawn on the day of *'Eid*. However, according to the Malik and ash-Shafi'i schools the *sadaqah* becomes obligatory at the setting of the sun on the last day of fasting, and that those who accept Islam or who are born after that are not due to pay it.

Though in the Hanafi school *sadaqah* becomes obligatory at dawn on the day of *'Eid*, according to some its purpose and spirit demand that it should be distributed among the poor and needy people a few days earlier so as to enable them to make necessary arrangements for their food and clothing well in time for the celebration of *'Eid* and congregational prayers. It is reported in Bukhari that the Companions of the Prophet usually paid out their *Sadaqat al-Fitr* a few days before *'Eid*. If a person cannot do so, he should distribute his *sadaqah* before *salat al-'Eid* in any case. The Prophet ﷺ has said:

> The sadaqah of the person who gives it away before the 'Eid Prayer will be accepted by Allah as real charity, but the sadaqah of the one who delays it and pays afterwards will be treated as ordinary charity. (Abu Dawud)

If someone forgets to pay off his *'Eid sadaqah* before *salat al-'Eid* due to negligence or some other reason, he must pay it as soon as possible after *salat al-'Eid*.

- A father has to pay *Sadaqat al-Fitr* not only for himself, but also for his minor children.
- A father also has to pay on behalf of his major children if they are poor and needy, otherwise not, except in the case of adult daughters who are as yet unmarried.
- A father has to pay on behalf of his insane children even if they are major whether or not they possess property.
- A master has to pay for his slaves, and for servants who are his dependants and living under his guardianship.
- In the Hanafi school a well-to-do woman has to pay *sadaqah*, but

only for herself; she is under no obligation to pay it on behalf of her children or parents or husband. If her husband does pay her *sadaqah* as an act of goodness it is permissible and valid. However, in the other schools the husband pays for his wife and for all his dependents.

) If the father is dead, the grandfather will pay the *sadaqah* on behalf of those mentioned above.

) *Sadaqat al-Fitr* is also obligatory for a person with a valid excuse who has not fasted during Ramadan.

Its amount is explained in the following hadith:

> *Ibn 'Umar ﷺ narrated that the Messenger of Allah ﷺ made the Sadaqat al-Fitr obligatory as a sa' of dates or a sa' of barley for slaves and free people, male and female, young and old of the Muslims.* (Bukhari)

(The *sa'* is a volume of four double handfuls. It is a volume of 2.03 litres, and will have a different weight according to the commodity in question.) Practically, the local mosque will advise the community of what this amounts to each year. *Sadaqat al-Fitr* must be given as wheat, barley, *sult* (a type of barley), dates, raisins, dried cottage cheese, rice, maize or millet, or according to the Hanafi *madhhab* its value can be given in cash.

The reasons for this *sadaqah* are two-fold.

> *Ibn Abbas reported: The Prophet ﷺ made Zakat al-Fitr obligatory as a purification for the fasting person from idle talk and indecent conversation and as food for the bereft. Whoever discharges it before the prayer, it is an accepted zakat, and whoever discharges it after the prayer, it is just a sadaqah.* (Abu Dawud)

Firstly, as with all *sadaqah*, it helps to wash away wrong actions.

Although, we may have devoted ourselves to the best of our abilities in *ibadah* during the month of Ramadan, we may unwittingly have committed some errors and the payment of this *sadaqah* helps to atone for those small mistakes and makes the fast complete. Secondly, it allows not only the wealthy people in a society to enjoy and celebrate *'Eid* but also the poor and needy, thus helping to foster love and harmony between all Muslims.

Salat al-'Eid

Salat al-'Eid is *sunnah* according to the majority of scholars and those who are obliged to attend the *Jumu'ah* ought to attend it, and there are differences of opinion as to those women, slaves and travellers who are not obliged to attend it. It is *wajib* (incumbent) according to Hanafi *fiqh* for men not women, adults not children, the healthy not the sick, residents not travellers and for the sane not the insane. The Prophet 🌼 performed it regularly and never missed it, as did the rightly guided *khulafa* and the great *imams* and jurists.

It is desirable to eat an odd number of dates and drink some water before leaving for the *'Eid al-Fitr* prayer. If dates are not available then anything else that is pure is acceptable. This is because the Prophet 🌼 did not eat on *'Eid al-Fitr* until he had eaten dates (Bukhari). It is recommended to take a bath, clean the teeth, wear perfume (men only) and to wear the best available clean clothes. It is recommended to walk to the *musalla* saying *takbir* and to return via a different route.

Salat al-'Eid should be performed in a public place, accessible to everyone and preferably an open space (*musalla*) outside of the town where the people of all the mosques in the town gather in one group under one imam. In difficult circumstances it may be prayed in the mosque. The congregation should consist of at least three people other than the imam. The time of *'Eid* prayer starts approximately thirty-five minutes after sunrise and lasts until noon. There is no *adhan* or *iqamah* for *'Eid* Prayer, which consists of two *rak'at*. Its distinguishing feature is the extra *takbirs*. After the prayer it is *sunnah* to remain sitting and to listen to the *khutbah*. It is *sunnah* for the imam to deliver two *khutbahs* after the *'Eid* prayer and teach people the rules about *Sadaqah al-Fitr* and remind people of the duties of that day. It is recommended for people to greet each other after the prayer. The Companions used to meet one another by saying, "May Allah accept it from us and from you."

OTHER OBLIGATORY AND OPTIONAL FASTS, AND FASTS THAT ARE FORBIDDEN

THE very nature of the understanding of Islam is to differentiate between what is obligatory and what is optional, and between what is forbidden and what is simply disliked but not forbidden. One must first attend to abandoning what is forbidden and to establishing the obligations, and then one can advance to doing those things that are recommended.

Forbidden Fasts

The only fasts that are forbidden are to fast on any of the *'Eid* days, except for people performing Hajj who may have to fast during the *'Eid al-Adha*. Those people who perform *tamattu'* Hajj and who do not sacrifice an animal should fast three days, adding another seven when they return to their homes. This is because Allah, exalted is He, says,

فَإِذَا أَمِنتُمْ فَمَن تَمَتَّعَ بِٱلْعُمْرَةِ إِلَى ٱلْحَجِّ فَمَا ٱسْتَيْسَرَ مِنَ ٱلْهَدْيِ فَمَن لَّمْ يَجِدْ فَصِيَامُ ثَلَٰثَةِ أَيَّامٍ فِي ٱلْحَجِّ وَسَبْعَةٍ إِذَا رَجَعْتُمْ تِلْكَ عَشَرَةٌ كَامِلَةٌ

If anyone wishes to continue the 'Umrah on to the Hajj, He must make an offering such as he can afford. But if he cannot afford it, he should fast three days during the Hajj and seven days on his return, making ten days in all. (2:196)

Disliked Fasts

It is permissible to fast on any other day of the year, but it is disliked to single out a Saturday or Sunday for fasting since they are the sacred days of the Jews and Christians. It is also disliked to fast every day without a break. Because of a well-known hadith some of the *'ulama* also disapprove of singling out Friday for fasting without joining either Thursday or Saturday to it. It is disapproved to fast on the day of doubt, which is the last day of Sha'ban, as a day of Ramadan when there is no decisive sighting of the moon confirmed by someone in authority.

Fard (Obligatory fasts)

These are only the fast of Ramadan.

Sunnah (Recommended Fasts)

'Ashura
The strongly confirmed *sunnah* (*mu'akkadah*) is the fast of *'Ashura* on the tenth of Muharram, although there is no wrong action if it is not

kept. It commemorates the Children of Israel and Musa ﷺ being saved from Fir'awn and the Egyptians.

> *Ibn Abbas said, "When the Prophet came to Madinah he found the Jews fasting 'Ashura. They were asked about it and they said, 'This is the day on which Allah gave Musa and the Children of Israel victory over Fir'awn, and we fast it in order to exalt it.' The Prophet, thereupon, said, 'we have more right to Musa than you,' and he gave the command to fast it.* (Bukhari)

Mustahabb (Recommended Fasts)

There are a number of different optional extra fasts that are well known in the *sunnah* and are recommended by the Prophet ﷺ and so are highly meritorious. Again, there is no wrong action if they are not kept.

The Sacred Months
This refers to fasting any or all of the four Sacred months – Dhu'l-Qa'dah, Dhu'l-Hijjah, Muharram and Rajab – and Sha'ban, the month immediately prior to Ramadan. Because this is an optional fast, it is permissible to leave it out entirely or do as much of it as is possible.

The First Ten Days of Dhu'l-Hijjah
It is especially meritorious to fast these ten days, often thought to be the ten mentioned in Surat al-Fajr:

$$وَٱلْفَجْرِ ۝ وَلَيَالٍ عَشْرٍ ۝$$
"By the dawn and ten nights." (89:1-2)

> *Hafsah ﷺ reported that the Prophet ﷺ used to fast the (first) nine days of Dhu'l–Hijjah. (An-Nasa'i, Ahmad and Abu Dawud)*

Yawm al-Arafah

Another well-known fast is the ninth of Dhu'l-Hijjah, the day of *'Arafah*. Abu Qatadah narrated that the Messenger of Allah ﷺ said:

> ... *Three days from every month, and Ramadan up to Ramadan: this is [equivalent to] fasting all the time. And fasting on 'Arafah, I anticipate from Allah that it will expiate the year before it and the year after it. And the fast of 'Ashura, I anticipate from Allah that it will expiate the year before it.* (Abu Dawud)

Just to fast these days carries such a tremendous reward that fasting the day of *'Arafah* makes up for the wrong actions not only of the previous year but also of the coming year, and *'Ashura* makes up for the wrong actions of the previous year.

Also the Prophet ﷺ clarified in this hadith that to fast Ramadan each year and to fast three days every month is equivalent to fasting continuously. That is because the reward of every good action is multiplied at least ten-fold, and so the three days in each month are equivalent to thirty days, i.e. to an entire month.

Six Days of Shawwal

By adding the six days of fasting during Shawwal to the fasting of Ramadan, the reward of a full year of fasting can be earned, insha'Allah. These fasts may be kept consecutively or at intervals during the month of Shawwal, i.e. spread out over the month.

> *Abu Ayyub* ﷺ *narrates that the Prophet* ﷺ *said, "Whoever fasted the full month of Ramadan and then follows it with the six fasts of Shawwal, is like a person who has fasted the full year."* (At-Targhib)

Mondays and Thursdays

It is also recommended to fast on Mondays and Thursdays since the Prophet ﷺ used to sometimes do this. When asked about it, he said:

Deeds are presented on every Monday and Thursday. Allah forgives every Muslim or every believer, except for those who shun each other. He says [about them]: 'Leave them.' (Ahmad)

Nafl (Voluntary Fasts)

A hadith that is a basis for action in respect to optional acts in general is that which Imam an-Nawawi included in his collection of Forty:

Abu Huraira ﷺ narrated that "The Messenger of Allah, may Allah bless him and grant him peace, said, 'Allah, exalted is He, said, "…My slave does not draw closer to Me with anything more beloved to Me than that which I have made obligatory upon him. My slave continues to draw closer to Me with optional extra acts until I love him."'"

Thus the most beloved act to Allah is what He has made an obligation for us. By doing extra after that, Muslims aspire to draw closer to Him.

Among the virtues of fasting is that Allah has designated one of the gates of the Garden solely for those who frequently fast. The Prophet ﷺ said:
"There is a gate in the Garden called ar-Rayyan, which those who fast will enter through on the Day of Rising, and none except them shall enter through it. It will be said, 'Where are those who used to fast?' They will stand up, and none except them will enter through it. Upon entry, that gate will be closed and no one else will enter through it." (Bukhari)

Therefore it is good practice not to forget fasting as an act of worship outside of Ramadan as well.

Reference:
Ibn Juzayy al-Kalbi, *Al-Qawanin al-Fiqhiyyah*, Dar al-Kitab al-Arabi, Beirut.